CANINE COOKING

This edition published by Parragon Books Ltd
in 2014 and distributed by

Parragon Inc.
440 Park Avenue South, 13th Floor
New York, NY 10016
www.parragon.com

Copyright © Parragon Books Ltd 2014
Produced by Tall Tree Ltd
Photography by Michael Wicks
Illustrations by the Apple Art Agency

ISBN 978-1-4723-3726-9

Printed in China

CANINE COOKING

Tasty treats for your four-legged friend

Shawn Sherry

PaRragon

Bath • New York • Singapore • Hong Kong • Cologne • Delhi
Melbourne • Amsterdam • Johannesburg • Shenzhen

Contents

Howl-iday fun recipes

Gourmet desserts

Allergen-free recipes

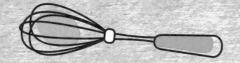

Home cooking is the perfect way to keep an eye on what your dog eats and to make sure they have a healthy and nutritious diet. Whether you're a master chef or just a pet lover, this cookbook will show you how to make delicious meals and treats that your dog will love.

Finding the ingredients

Most of the ingredients used in the recipes in this book can be bought from local grocery stores and supermarkets. A few, such as carob chips and dried apple pieces, can be obtained from health-food stores and online food suppliers.

How much food?

This depends on your dog's size and lifestyle. Some recipes will make one meal for a large dog but up to four for a smaller one. Some recipes are entire meals, but others are for treats or snacks, which should be eaten in small amounts, in addition to regular meals.

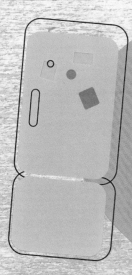

Storage

To make sure that your home-cooked food lasts longer, keep it in an airtight plastic container or a ziplock bag before putting it into the refrigerator or freezer. Storage times can be found at the end of each recipe.

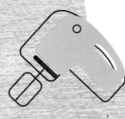

Food allergies

You may discover that your pet pooch finds it hard to stomach certain foods, such as those containing wheat. The final section of this book contains a few allergen-free recipes to satisfy the most sensitive of stomachs. If you are uncertain how your dog will tolerate any of the ingredients, then please consult your veterinarian.

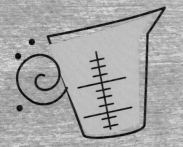

PLEASE DON'T FEED ME ONIONS, CHOCOLATE, AVOCADO, RAISINS, GRAPES, OR THE SEEDS OF ANY FRUITS, BECAUSE THEY CAN HARM ME.

CHAPTER 1

Tail-waggin' meat
lovers' recipes

OVEN
MEASURING CUPS
LARGE MIXING BOWL
MIXING SPOON
ROLLING PIN
SHAPED CUTTER
BAKING SHEET

CHEESEBURGER CHOW

INGREDIENTS

5 CUPS ROLLED OATS

1 CUP BEEF STOCK

¾ CUP GRATED PARMESAN CHEESE

1 Preheat the oven to 375°F.

2 Pour the oats and stock into the bowl and mix together until thoroughly combined.

3 Slowly add the Parmesan cheese to the oat mixture and mix well to combine.

4 Put the oat mixture onto a clean surface and roll it out until it is about ½ inch thick.

5 Cut out as many shapes as you can, depending on the size of your cutter, and place them on the baking sheet. Bake for about 30 minutes.

6 Let the shapes cool before serving to your pup.

7 The shapes can be kept in the refrigerator for up to two weeks.

POULTRY PERFECTION

EQUIPMENT

OVEN
BAKING PAN
LIQUID MEASURING CUP
TWO SAUCEPANS
MEASURING CUPS
VEGETABLE PEELER
CUTTING BOARD
KNIFE
LARGE MIXING BOWL
MIXING SPOON

1 Preheat the oven to 350°F. Place the chicken in the baking pan and cook it for about 30 minutes, or until the chicken is completely cooked and the meat is no longer pink.

2 Bring 1½ cups of the water to a boil in a saucepan, then pour in the rice. Let the rice cook over a low heat for 45 minutes or until the water is completely absorbed.

3 Peel the carrot, then chop the carrot and green beans into small pieces and add the peas. Put the vegetables and the remaining water into a separate saucepan and boil them for 5 minutes.

4 Place the cooked chicken onto the cutting board and cut it into small cubes.

5 Put the chicken, rice, and vegetables into the bowl and mix together until thoroughly combined.

6 Let the mixture cool to room temperature before serving to your pup.

7 This will make 1–4 servings, depending on the size of your dog. It can be kept in the refrigerator for two days, or frozen for up to one month.

INGREDIENTS

1 LARGE, BONELESS CHICKEN BREAST (ABOUT 8 OUNCES)

2½ CUPS WATER

¾ CUP RICE

2 SMALL CARROTS

1 CUP GREEN BEANS

½ CUP PEAS

STRAWBERRY PUP-SICLES

1 Cut 4 ounces of strawberries into quarters, slicing off the stems (you should have about ¾ cup), and put them into a blender.

2 Pour ½ cup of water into a blender and blend the ingredients until they form a smooth mixture.

3 Pour the strawberry mixture into a 6-10 compartment ice cube tray and put it in a freezer until frozen. These are great to bring along to a picnic to help your pup keep cool in the heat.

Picnic treats

Alfresco dining is absolutely paw-fect!

READY FOR THE PICNIC

TAIL MIX

1 Preheat the oven to 300°F. Cut an apple, pear, banana, and carrot into thin slices. Put the slices onto a baking sheet.

2 Bake them in the oven for 30 minutes.

3 Turn the slices over and bake for an additional 30 minutes or until the slices feel dry.

4 Let the slices cool before serving to your pup. The slices can be kept in the refrigerator for a week.

ONE FISH, CHEW FISH

EQUIPMENT

OVEN
MEASURING CUPS
LARGE MIXING BOWL
MIXING SPOON
ROLLING PIN
SHAPED CUTTER
BAKING SHEET

1 Preheat the oven to 375°F.

2 Pour the oats and stock into the bowl and mix together until thoroughly combined.

3 Slowly add the Parmesan cheese to the oat mixture and mix well to combine.

4 Put the oat mixture onto a clean surface and roll it out until it is about ½ inch thick.

5 Cut out as many shapes as you can, depending on the size of your cutter, and place them on the baking sheet. Bake for about 30 minutes.

6 Let the shapes cool before serving to your pup.

7 The shapes can be kept in the refrigerator for up to two weeks.

INGREDIENTS

5 CUPS ROLLED OATS

1 CUP FISH STOCK

¾ CUP GRATED PARMESAN CHEESE

16

BACON BONE-ANZA

EQUIPMENT

OVEN
SKILLET
PAPER TOWELS
CUTTING BOARD
KNIFE
MEASURING CUPS
LARGE MIXING BOWL
MIXING SPOON
12 CUPCAKE LINERS
12-HOLE CUPCAKE PAN

1 Preheat the oven to 375°F.

2 Cook the bacon in the skillet for 10 minutes or until it is crispy.

3 Let the bacon drain on paper towels, before putting it onto the cutting board and cutting it into small pieces.

4 Put the rolled oats, bacon, and honey into the bowl and mix together until thoroughly combined.

5 Place 12 cupcake liners into the pan and scoop the mixture into the liners, filling each one to the top.

6 Bake in the oven for about 20 minutes, or until the tops are crunchy.

7 Let the cupcakes cool before serving to your pup.

8 The cupcakes can be kept in the refrigerator for up to four days.

INGREDIENTS

2 STRIPS OF BACON

5 CUPS ROLLED OATS

¼ CUP HONEY

CHAPTER 2

Two-paws-up
veggie recipes

POOCH SALAD

EQUIPMENT

MEASURING CUPS
VEGETABLE PEELER
CUTTING BOARD
KNIFE
LARGE MIXING BOWL
MIXING SPOON

1 Wash the lettuce and peel the cucumber, carrot, and sweet potato.

2 Cut the cucumber, carrot, and sweet potato into cubes, measuring about ½ inch across, and put them into the bowl.

3 Chop the lettuce into small pieces and add these to the bowl.

4 Pour the yogurt into the bowl and stir the ingredients until everything has been coated thoroughly. Feed the salad to your pup immediately.

5 This will make 1–4 servings, depending on the size of your dog. It can be be kept in the refrigerator for two days.

INGREDIENTS

½ SMALL HEAD OF LETTUCE

½ CUCUMBER

3 SMALL OR 2 MEDIUM CARROTS

1 SMALL SWEET POTATO

¼ CUP LOW-FAT YOGURT

Healthy rewards

Tasty treats to keep your pup in tip-top condition.

GO FETCH CELERY STICKS

1 Cut the leaves off the top of three celery stalks and cut each stick into pieces about 4 inches long.

2 Spread peanut butter into the inner channel of each celery stalk.

3 Serve as a healthy snack.

FRUIT PUPS

1. Core an apple, then cut the apple, a banana, and ⅓ cup of hulled strawberries into small cubes.

2. Put the fruit cubes into a bowl and mix with ½ cup of blueberries. Serve the fruit pup to your dog.

TIP

Boil the fruit in some water for 5 minutes to soften it a little if your pup likes food to be a little less crunchy.

A HEALTHY BEACH RUN

PAW-PKIN PIE

EQUIPMENT

OVEN
MEASURING CUPS
LARGE MIXING BOWL
MIXING SPOON
ROLLING PIN
KNIFE OR LARGE
ROUND CUTTER
12-HOLE CUPCAKE PAN

1 Preheat the oven to 375°F.

2 Put the flour, water, and ⅝ cup of pumpkin puree into the mixing bowl.

3 Mix the ingredients together thoroughly to form a dough. Place the dough onto a clean surface and roll out until it is about ¼ inch thick.

4 Cut the dough into 12 circles, measuring about 6 inches across, using the knife or cutter.

5 Place the circles into the sections of the cupcake pan, making sure that some excess dough sits above each cupcake section.

6 Put a spoonful of the remaining pumpkin puree into each well. Then take the excess dough around the edges of each cupcake well and pinch each pie closed, to form a package.

7 Bake the pies for 30 minutes, or until the top of each pie has browned slightly.

8 Let the pies cool before serving to your pup.

9 The pies can be kept in the refrigerator for up to four days.

INGREDIENTS

3½ CUPS ALL-PURPOSE FLOUR

½ CUP WATER

1½ CUPS PUMPKIN PUREE

26

LIQUID MEASURING CUP
TWO SAUCEPANS
MEASURING CUPS
VEGETABLE PEELER
CUTTING BOARD
KNIFE
MIXING SPOON
LARGE MIXING BOWL

BOW-WOW VEGGIE DELIGHT

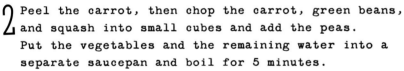

1 Bring 1½ cups of the water to a boil in a saucepan, then pour in the rice. Let the rice cook over low heat for 45 minutes, or until the water is completely absorbed.

2 Peel the carrot, then chop the carrot, green beans, and squash into small cubes and add the peas. Put the vegetables and the remaining water into a separate saucepan and boil for 5 minutes.

3 Chop the cucumber into small cubes.

4 Pour the rice, carrots, green beans, squash, peas, and cucumber into the bowl and mix them together thoroughly.

5 Let the mixture cool to room temperature before serving to your pup.

6 This will make 1–4 servings, depending on the size of your dog. It can be kept in the refrigerator for two days, or frozen for up to one month.

INGREDIENTS

2½ cups WATER

¾ cups RICE

2 small CARROTS

1 cup GREEN BEANS

¼ OF A BUTTERNUT SQUASH

¼ cup PEAS

⅓ OF A CUCUMBER

CHAPTER 3

Howl-iday
fun recipes

CANINE CARROT EASTER COOKIES

1 Preheat the oven to 375°F.

2 Peel the carrot and cut it into small pieces. Put the pieces into the blender and add the water.

3 Blend the ingredients thoroughly until they form a smooth mixture.

4 Pour the oats and carrot mixture into the bowl and mix them together thoroughly.

5 Put the oat mixture onto a clean surface and roll it out until it is about ½ inch thick.

6 Cut out as many Easter shapes as you can, depending on the size of your cutter, and place them on the baking sheet.

7 Bake the cookies for 30 minutes, or until they are hard, then let them cool before serving to your pup.

8 The cookies can be kept in the refrigerator for up to two weeks.

EQUIPMENT

OVEN
MEASURING CUPS
VEGETABLE PEELER
CUTTING BOARD
KNIFE
BLENDER
LARGE MIXING BOWL
MIXING SPOON
ROLLING PIN
EASTER EGG-SHAPED CUTTER
BAKING SHEET

INGREDIENTS

3 LARGE CARROTS

1 CUP WATER

5 CUPS ROLLED OATS

TURKEY DINNER

1 Preheat the oven to 350°F. Put the turkey into the baking pan and cook it for about 30 minutes, or until the turkey is completely cooked and the meat is no longer pink.

2 Bring 1¾ cups of the water to a boil in a saucepan, then pour in the rice. Let the rice cook over low heat for 45 minutes, or until the water is completely absorbed.

3 Peel the carrot, then chop the carrot and green beans into small pieces and add the peas. Put the vegetables and the remaining water into a separate saucepan and boil them for 5 minutes.

4 Place the cooked turkey onto the cutting board and cut it into small cubes.

5 Put the turkey, rice, vegetables, and cranberries into the bowl and mix together until thoroughly combined.

6 Let the mixture cool to room temperature before serving to your pup.

7 This will make 1–4 servings, depending on the size of your dog. It can be kept in the refrigerator for two days, or frozen for up to one month.

WOOF

EQUIPMENT

OVEN
MEASURING CUPS
BAKING PAN
LIQUID MEASURING CUPS
TWO SAUCEPANS
VEGETABLE PEELER
CUTTING BOARD
KNIFE
LARGE MIXING BOWL
MIXING SPOON

INGREDIENTS

1 LARGE, BONELESS TURKEY BREAST (ABOUT 8 OUNCES)

2½ cups WATER

¾ cup RICE

2 SMALL CARROTS

1 cup GREEN BEANS

⅓ cup PEAS

⅓ cup DRIED CRANBERRIES

EQUIPMENT

OVEN
MEASURING CUPS
LARGE MIXING BOWL
MIXING SPOON
ROLLING PIN
HEART-SHAPE CUTTERS
BAKING SHEET

HONEY HEART COOKIES

1 Preheat the oven to 375°F.

2 Pour the rolled oats, honey, and water into the bowl and mix together until thoroughly combined.

3 Put the oat mixture onto a clean surface and roll it out until it is about ½ inch thick.

4 Cut out as many shapes as you can, depending on the size of your cutter, and place them on the baking sheet. Bake for about 30 minutes.

5 Let the cookies cool before serving to your pup.

6 The cookies can be kept in the refrigerator for up to two weeks.

INGREDIENTS

5 CUPS ROLLED OATS

½ CUP HONEY

1 CUP WATER

SCARY SWEET POTATO CRUNCH

1 Preheat the oven to 375°F.

2 Peel the sweet potato and cut it into small pieces. Put the pieces into the blender, add the water, and blend the ingredients until they form a smooth mixture.

3 Pour the oats and the sweet potato mixture into the bowl and mix them together thoroughly.

4 Put the oat mixture onto a clean surface and roll it out until it is about ½ inch thick.

5 Cut out as many Halloween shapes as you can, depending on the size of your cutters, and place them on the baking sheet. Bake the shapes for 30 minutes, or until they are hard.

6 Let the shapes cool before serving to your pup. Once cool, you can make small holes and decorate the cookies with the dried cranberries.

7 The shapes can be kept in the refrigerator for up to two weeks.

EQUIPMENT

OVEN
MEASURING CUPS
VEGETABLE PEELER
CUTTING BOARD
KNIFE
BLENDER
LARGE MIXING BOWL
MIXING SPOON
ROLLING PIN
HALLOWEEN-SHAPE CUTTERS
BAKING SHEET

INGREDIENTS

1 LARGE SWEET POTATO

1 CUP WATER

5 CUPS ROLLED OATS

DRIED CRANBERRIES FOR DECORATION

Birthday parties

Helpful hints for the perfect pooch party.

CAROB-COVERED PAWBERRIES

1 Put 1 cup of carob chips into a microwavable cup and pour 2 tablespoons of canola oil over the top.

2 Put the cup into a microwave and heat on full power for 1 minute, or until the carob has melted.

3 Dip strawberries into the melted carob, so that they are half covered, and place them on a sheet of wax paper.

4 Put the strawberries in a refrigerator and serve once the carob has hardened.

WHAT'S THAT IN DOG YEARS?

BIRTHDAY BREAKFAST PUPMEAL

1 Core an apple and cut it into small cubes.

2 Pour 1 cup of water into a ceramic bowl and put it in a microwave on full power for 2 minutes.

3 Take the warm water from the microwave and pour it on top of 2½ cups of rolled oats.

4 Stir the ingredients until the water has been absorbed into the oats.

5 Mix the chopped apple and ½ cup of fresh blueberries into the oatmeal. Let the mixture cool and then serve.

BIRTHDAY PUP-CAKES

EQUIPMENT

OVEN
MEASURING CUPS
BLENDER
LARGE MIXING BOWL
MIXING SPOON
12 CUPCAKE LINERS
12-HOLE CUPCAKE PAN
KITCHEN SPOON

1 Preheat the oven to 375°F.

2 Wash the cherries and put ⅔ cup of them into the blender. Add the water.

3 Blend the ingredients together until they form a smooth mixture.

4 Pour the oats and the cherry mixture into the bowl and mix them together thoroughly.

5 Place 12 cupcake liners into the cupcake pan. Scoop the oat and cherry mixture into the liners, filling them to the top.

6 Place a half cherry on top of each cupcake.

7 Bake the cupcakes for about 20 minutes, or until the tops are crunchy.

8 Let the cupcakes cool before serving to your pup.

9 The cupcakes can be kept in the refrigerator for up to four days.

INGREDIENTS

1 CUP PITTED CHERRIES

1 CUP WATER

5 CUPS ROLLED OATS

BLUEBERRY BIRTHDAY CAKE

1 Preheat the oven to 375°F.

2 Wash the blueberries and put them into the blender with the peeled banana and the water. Blend the ingredients thoroughly until they form a smooth mixture.

3 Pour the oats and the blueberry mixture into the bowl and mix them together thoroughly.

4 Use your hands to roll the mixture to create one large ball and three smaller ones.

5 Place the larger ball onto the baking sheet, pushing down to flatten it slightly.

6 Place the smaller balls onto the baking sheet around the top of the larger ball to create a paw-print shape. Again, push down to flatten the smaller balls a little.

7 Bake the cake for 30 minutes, or until the top of the cake is slightly crunchy.

8 Let the cake cool before serving slices to your pup.

9 The cake can be kept in the refrigerator for up to four days.

EQUIPMENT

OVEN
MEASURING CUPS
BLENDER
LARGE MIXING BOWL
MIXING SPOON
BAKING SHEET

INGREDIENTS

1½ CUPS BLUEBERRIES

1 BANANA

1 CUP WATER

5 CUPS ROLLED OATS

CHAPTER 4

Gourmet desserts

PEANUT BUTTER POOCH BITES

EQUIPMENT

OVEN
MEASURING CUPS
LARGE MIXING BOWL
MIXING SPOON
BROWNIE BAKING PAN
SPATULA
LARGE MICROWAVABLE CUP
MICROWAVE

1 Preheat the oven to 375°F.

2 Put the rolled oats, peanut butter, and water into the bowl and mix them together thoroughly.

3 Scoop the mixture into the baking pan and smooth the surface, using the spatula.

4 Bake for 30 minutes, or until the top is slightly crunchy, and let it cool.

5 Put the carob chips into the microwavable cup and pour the canola oil on top.

6 Heat in the microwave at full power for 1 minute 20 seconds. Take the cup out of the microwave and mix the melted carob and oil until they are thoroughly combined.

7 Pour the carob mixture over the top of the peanut-butter bars and use the spatula to smooth the surface.

8 Put the baking pan in the refrigerator to harden the carob. Cut the mixture into small bars before serving to your pup.

9 The bars can be kept in the refrigerator for four days, or in the freezer for one month.

INGREDIENTS

5 cups ROLLED OATS

½ cup PEANUT BUTTER

1 cup WATER

1¼ cups CAROB CHIPS

¼ cup CANOLA OIL

CAROB PEANUT BUTTER PUPS

EQUIPMENT

MEASURING CUPS
LARGE MICROWAVABLE CUP
MICROWAVE
MIXING SPOON
12 CUPCAKE LINERS
12-HOLE CUPCAKE PAN
KITCHEN SPOONS

1. Put the carob chips into the microwavable cup and pour the canola oil on top.

2. Heat in the microwave at full power for 1 minute 20 seconds. Take the cup out of the microwave and mix the melted carob and oil until they are thoroughly combined.

3. Place 12 cupcake liners into the cupcake pan. Put a spoonful of melted carob into the cupcake cases and smooth the inside of each to create a hollow carob shell.

4. Put the cupcake pan into the refrigerator for 2 hours, or until the carob is hard.

5. Put a spoonful of peanut butter into each carob shell and press down, so that it does not stick out above the top of the cupcake liner.

6. Pour the remaining melted carob on top of each cupcake so that the peanut butter is covered.

7. Put the cupcake pan back into the refrigerator to harden the carob before serving to your pup.

8. The cupcakes can be kept in the refrigerator for four days, or in the freezer for up to a month.

INGREDIENTS

1¼ cups CAROB CHIPS

¼ cup CANOLA OIL

½ cup PEANUT BUTTER

Sweet treats

Try these simple treats on your favorite hound.

FROZEN BANANA TREATS

1 Mash two bananas and put them into a bowl with ¼ cup of peanut butter and 2 cups of low-fat vanilla yogurt.

2 Mix the ingredients until they are thoroughly combined.

3 Pour the mixture into a 24 compartment ice cube tray and put it in a freezer. Wait until the treats have frozen before serving to your pup.

TIP

Put the peanut butter in a microwave to melt it a little and make it easier to mix.

APPLE CRUNCH CAKES

SWEET TOOTH

1 Preheat the oven to 350°F.

2 Put 2½ cups of water, ¼ cup of applesauce, 2 tablespoons of honey, a large egg, and a drop of vanilla extract into a bowl. Mix the ingredients until they are thoroughly combined.

3 Add 2 cups of wholewheat flour, 1 cup of dried apple pieces, and 2½ teaspoons of baking powder. Mix the ingredients until they are thoroughly combined.

4 Put the mixture into the sections of a 12-hole cupcake pan and bake in the oven for 1 hour and 15 minutes. Let the cakes cool before serving to your pup.

BLUEBERRY COOKIES

1 Preheat the oven to 375°F.

2 Wash the blueberries and put them into the blender with the peeled banana and the water. Blend the ingredients together until they form a smooth mixture.

3 Pour the flour and the blueberry mixture into the bowl. Mix the ingredients together to form a dough. Transfer the dough onto the baking sheet, shaping it with your hands to create a loaf about 2 inches high.

4 Bake for 20 minutes, or until the top of the loaf feels firm.

5 Take the loaf out of the oven and let it cool on the cutting board. Cut the loaf into cookies that are ½ inch thick.

6 Place the cookies onto the baking sheet and put them back into the oven for 20 minutes. Turn each cookie over and bake for another 20 minutes. Take the cookies out and let them cool.

7 Put the carob chips into the microwavable cup and pour the canola oil on top.

8 Heat in the microwave at full power for 1 minute 20 seconds. Take the cup out of the microwave and mix the melted carob and oil until they are thoroughly combined.

9 Dunk the end of each cookie into the melted carob and place onto the cool baking sheet. Put the baking sheet into the refrigerator to harden the carob before serving to your pup.

10 The cookies can be kept in the refrigerator for four days, or in the freezer for up to one month.

EQUIPMENT

OVEN
MEASURING CUPS
BLENDER
LARGE MIXING BOWL
MIXING SPOON
BAKING SHEET
CUTTING BOARD
KNIFE
LARGE MICROWAVABLE CUP
MICROWAVE

INGREDIENTS

1½ CUPS BLUEBERRIES

1 BANANA

1 CUP WATER

3⅔ CUPS ALL-PURPOSE FLOUR

1¼ CUPS CAROB CHIPS

1 CUP CANOLA OIL

CHAPTER 5

Allergen-free recipes

SWEET POTATO CHIPS

EQUIPMENT

OVEN
CUTTING BOARD
KNIFE
BAKING SHEET

1 Preheat the oven to 325°F.

2 Wash the sweet potatoes and put them onto the cutting board. Cut the sweet potatoes into thin slices.

3 Put the sweet potato slices onto the baking sheet and bake them for about 30 minutes.

4 Turn the slices over and put them back into the oven for another 30 minutes, or until the slices feel crunchy.

5 Take the slices out of the oven and let them cool before serving to your pup.

6 The chips can be kept in the refrigerator for up to seven days, or in the freezer for up to one month.

INGREDIENTS

2 LARGE SWEET POTATOES

OVEN
MEASURING CUPS
CUTTING BOARD
KNIFE
BLENDER
LARGE MIXING BOWL
MIXING SPOON
ROLLING PIN
SHAPED CUTTER
BAKING SHEET

PEAR AND BANANA COOKIES

1 Preheat the oven to 375°F.

2 Wash the pear and cut it into small pieces. Put the pieces into the blender with the peeled banana and the water.

3 Blend the ingredients together until they form a smooth mixture.

4 Put the pear mixture and the oats into the bowl and mix the ingredients together until they are thoroughly combined.

5 Put the oat mixture onto a clean surface and roll it out until it is about ½ inch thick.

6 Cut out as many shapes as you can, depending on the size of your cutter, and place them on the baking sheet.

7 Bake for 30 minutes, or until the cookies are hard. Let them cool before serving to your pup.

8 The cookies can be kept in the refrigerator for up to two weeks.

INGREDIENTS

1 LARGE FRESH PEAR

1 BANANA

1 CUP WATER

5 CUPS GLUTEN-FREE ROLLED OATS

DUCK DELIGHT

1. Preheat the oven to 425°F. Place the duck breast in the baking pan and put it in the oven for 8 minutes.

2. Check that the bottom of the duck breast has browned. Turn the breast over and cook for another 8 minutes. Check that the duck is cooked thoroughly and the meat is no longer pink.

3. Put the breast onto the cutting board and cut it into cubes about 1 inch in size.

4. Bring 1¾ cups of the water to a boil in a saucepan, then pour in the rice. Let the rice cook on a low heat for 45 minutes, or until the water is completely absorbed.

5. Peel the carrot and squash and chop the carrot, squash, and green beans into small cubes, then add the peas. Put the vegetables and the remaining water into a separate saucepan and boil them for 5 minutes.

6. Put the duck, rice, and vegetables into the bowl and mix together until thoroughly combined.

7. Let the mixture cool to room temperature before serving to your pup.

8. This will make 1-4 servings, depending on the size of your dog. It can also be kept in the refrigerator for two days, or frozen for up to one month.

EQUIPMENT

OVEN
MEASURING CUPS
BAKING PAN
CUTTING BOARD
KNIFE
LIQUID MEASURING CUP
TWO SAUCEPANS
VEGETABLE PEELER
LARGE MIXING BOWL
MIXING SPOON

INGREDIENTS

1 LARGE DUCK BREAST
(ABOUT 8 OUNCES)

2½ CUPS WATER

¾ CUP RICE

2 SMALL CARROTS

½ OF A BUTTERNUT SQUASH

1 CUP GREEN BEANS

⅓ CUP PEAS

INDEX